THE GREAT SCIENTISTS

ISAAC NEWTON

Kavita Sharma and Aaliya Roy Kundal

Om KIDZ
An imprint of Om Books International

Have you ever wondered why a ball comes down after you throw it up in the air?

Why doesn't it zoom into space even if you throw it up with great force? A great scientist called Isaac Newton explained why.

Newton, as he is better known, was born on 25 December 1642 in a village called Woolsthorpe in England. *(Interesting fact: Another great scientist, Galileo Galilei, died the same year.)* Netwon was born a very weak baby and wasn't expected to live. But he lived to the ripe old age of 84!

Newton spent most of his childhood with his grandmother. He did his initial classes at a small school in Woolsthorpe village. When Newton was 11 years old, he was sent to a town called Grantham to study at King's school. There he lived with Mr Clark, who was a pharmacist (one who makes and gives out medicines). Mr Clark had a laboratory that young Newton spent much time in, tinkering with tools to build small machines like floating lanterns, a water clock and even a windmill run by a live mouse.

When Newton turned 16, his mother brought him back to Woolsthorpe to take care of her farm. But he was terrible at it. When he was supposed to be herding cattle, he would sit under a tree with a book. Newton's mother realised he hated farming and sent him back to school.

After a few more years of schooling, Newton was ready for college. He joined the famous Trinity College in Cambridge. There he studied natural philosophy, which is the study of nature and universe.

While at Cambridge, Newton worked hard on his own course but also read about philosophers and scientists like Aristotle and René Descartes. He learnt what they had said about how the world works. Newton completed his bachelor's degree in 1665 and wanted to study more. But Cambridge closed in 1665 due to the Great Plague, a deadly disease that killed thousands of people in London.

Newton returned to Woolsthorpe for about two years, spending his time thinking and conducting small experiments. This is the time he thought of his most famous idea: gravity, which is the invisible force that pulls objects towards each other. It is the gravity of the Earth that makes a ball come down after you throw it up.

The story is that Newton came up with this idea while sitting under an apple tree. He saw how apples always fall straight to the ground. They never go sideways or upwards. This inspired him to study the matter further, and he formed the theory of gravity.

When Cambridge reopened in 1667, Newton went back to study for a master's degree. In 1668, he built a reflecting telescope using mirrors instead of lenses. His mathematics professor, Isaac Barrow, was so impressed with his telescope that he took it to the Royal Society of London, the most respected society of scientists in England. They were very impressed too.

Newton began writing his most important book, known as *Principia,* in 1684. It was published in 1687. In the *Principia,* he wrote about the three laws of motion. These laws of motion explain the movement of objects and how the movement can be affected by various things.

He also wrote about the Universal Law of Gravitation, which explained that all objects and planets in the universe are attracted towards each other by a force called gravitation. The Earth keeps revolving around the Sun because of the Sun's force of gravitation.

$$F = \frac{Gm_1m_2}{r^2}$$

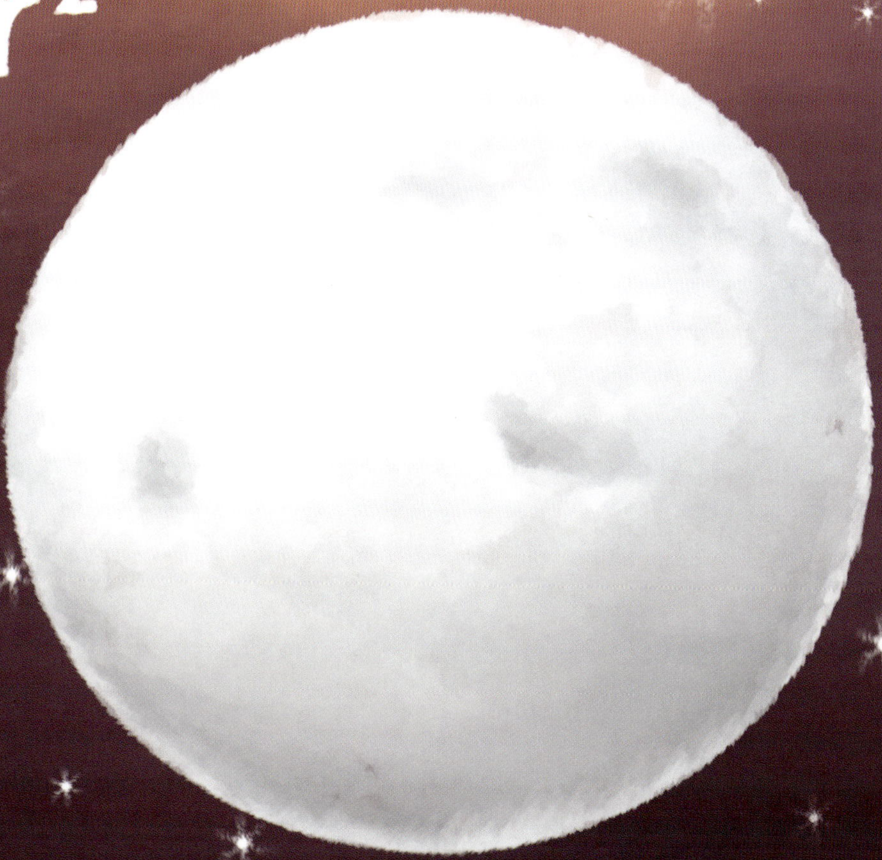

In 1704, Newton published his book called *Opticks,* which talked about light. Newton discovered that white light is made up of seven colours: violet, indigo, blue, green, yellow, orange, and red. These are the colours of the rainbow! Rainbows are formed when white light from the Sun shines through drops of rain and bends to show the seven colours.

All his work and great theories had made Newton very famous. He was knighted by Queen Anne in 1705. Knighthood is the highest honour that can be given to anyone in the United Kingdom. Newton was now called Sir Isaac Newton.

Newton died on 20 March 1727. He was buried at Westminster Abbey, London, where many other famous people like Charles Darwin, Charles Dickens and Rudyard Kipling are also buried.

Newton was one of the greatest scientists in history. Even Albert Einstein, another great scientist, acknowledged said that Newton was the smartest person to have lived. He influenced modern science and formed the basis for modern physics. Newton's scientific legacy will inspire us forever.

What we know is a drop, what we don't know is an ocean.

– Isaac Newton